D1505893

WHEN DINOSAURS LIVED

Triceratops

KATE RIGGS

Published by
CREATIVE EDUCATION

P.O. Box 227, Mankato, Minnesota 56002
Creative Education is an imprint of The Creative Company
www.thecreativecompany.us

Design and production by Danny Nanos of Gilbert & Nanos
Art direction by Rita Marshall
Printed by Corporate Graphics in the United States of America

Photographs by Alamy (INTERFOTO), Bridgeman Art Library (O. Cenig,
Peter Snowball), Corbis (Louie Psihoyos, Bill Varie), Dreamstime (Peterpolak), Getty Images
(DEA Picture Library, De Agostini), iStockphoto (Kickers), Library of Congress

Library of Congress Cataloging-in-Publication Data
Riggs, Kate.
Triceratops / by Kate Riggs.
p. cm.
Summary: A brief introduction to the horned *Triceratops*,
highlighting its size, habitat, food sources, and demise. Also included is a
virtual field trip to a museum with notable *Triceratops* fossils.

Includes bibliographical references and index.

ISBN 978-1-60818-119-3

1. Triceratops—Juvenile literature. I. Title.

QE862.O65R5565 2012

567.915'8—dc22   2010049333

CPSIA: 031412 PO1557

2 4 6 8 9 7 5 3

CREATIVE EDUCATION

Table of Contents

Triceratops was a ceratopsid dinosaur. It lived from 68 to 65 million years ago. The name *Triceratops* means "three-horned face."

Triceratops is known mainly for its three horns

At 10 feet (3 m) tall and 30 feet (9 m) long, *Triceratops* was a big dinosaur! It had three horns on its face and a frill around its head. *Triceratops* could charge at predators with its sharp horns.

Triceratops charged at enemies like modern rhinos do today

After it hatched, *Triceratops* grew quickly. An adult dinosaur weighed about 6 tons (5.4 t). A big *Triceratops* could run as fast as 25 miles (40 km) an hour if something was chasing it! It could also stand up on its back legs to scare away a predator.

Torosaurus was another ceratopsid about the size of *Triceratops*

Triceratops lived in or near forests. The forests had plenty of ferns, cycads, and bushy evergreen shrubs to eat. The first maple, oak, and walnut trees appeared when *Triceratops* was alive. But the dinosaur was not tall enough to reach those leaves.

Triceratops used its pointy mouth, called a beak, to eat plants

Herds of *Triceratops* wandered around, finding plants to eat. They ate all day long. Other plant-eaters like the duck-billed *Edmontosaurus* lived nearby. Meat-eaters such as *Tyrannosaurus rex* tried to eat *Triceratops*.

A pair of *Tyrannosaurus* hunters could take down *Triceratops*

A group of ceratopsids protected each other from meat-eating predators. But sometimes a hungry *T. rex* was too strong for them. *Triceratops* died out about 65 million years ago. All the dinosaurs disappeared then.

All that is left of *Triceratops* today are its bones

Scientists know about *Triceratops* because they have studied fossils. Fossils are the remains of living things that died long ago. Many fossils of *Triceratops* have been found in the western United States. The first one was found in 1888.

A man named John Bell Hatcher found the first *Triceratops* skull

Triceratops compared
with a five-foot-tall
(152 cm) person

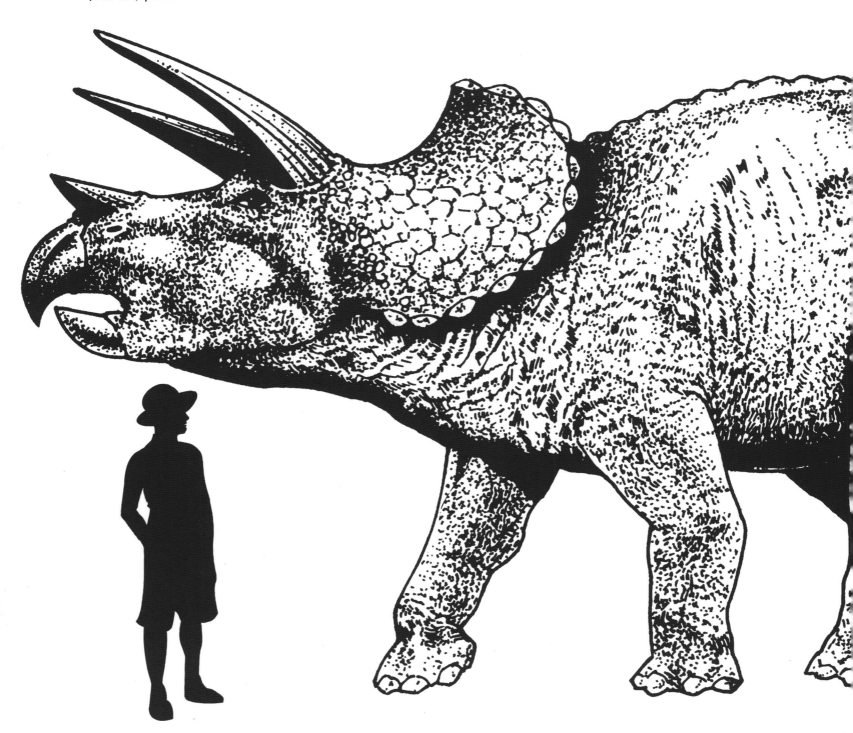

Paleontologists are people who study dinosaurs. Othniel C. Marsh was the paleontologist who named *Triceratops*. He called it "three-horned face" because of the three horns that stick out from the dinosaur's face.

SOUND IT OUT

paleontologists: *pay-lee-ahn-TAHL-oh-jists*

People used to think that *Triceratops* used its frill to scare away predators. Now people think that the frill also helped *Triceratops* keep its body cool or warm. But scientists still study *Triceratops*. There are more things to learn about this "three-horned face"!

Some people think *Triceratops* had colors on its frill

A Virtual Field Trip: Smithsonian Institution, Washington, D.C.

You can see a *Triceratops* skeleton at the Smithsonian Institution in Washington, D.C. In 1905, the skeleton was pieced together from parts of many different dinosaurs. It was the first *Triceratops* ever displayed in a museum. In the 1990s, paleontologists took it apart and replaced some of the bones that did not fit. The new and improved *Triceratops* has been on display since 2001.

Glossary

ceratopsid—a four-legged, plant-eating dinosaur that had a horned head and a bony frill protecting the neck

cycads—plants that look like palm trees and have big cones, or dry fruit

evergreen—green all the time; evergreen plants have leaves that stay green year round

frill—a bony plate that curved up behind the head of a ceratopsid

hatched—came out of an egg

predators—animals that kill and eat other animals

Bones from different *Triceratops* are often used to make a skeleton

Read More

Dixon, Dougal. *Plant-eating Dinosaurs*.
Mankato, Minn.: NewForest Press, 2011.

Johnson, Jinny. *Triceratops and Other Horned and Armored Dinosaurs*.
North Mankato, Minn.: Smart Apple Media, 2008.

Web Sites

Dinosaur Facts
http://www.thelearningpage.org/dinosaurs/dinosaur_facts.htm
This site has a fact sheet about *Triceratops* that can be printed out.

Enchanted Learning: Triceratops
http://www.enchantedlearning.com/subjects/dinosaurs/dinos/Triceratops.shtml
This site has *Triceratops* facts and a picture to color.